*For Alessandro Bianchi (Cantù, Italy)*

# Three American Songs

Arranged by
Hans Uwe Hielscher

Amazing Grace

Somebody's Knocking at Your Door

Deep River

op.51

## H. T. FitzSimons Company

*One of the Fred Bock Companies*

Exclusively Distributed by
Hal•Leonard

# AMAZING GRACE

Sw.   Gambe 8', Voix Celeste 8'
Gt.    Flute Harmonique 8'
Ped.  Subbass 16', Sw./Ped.

Traditional
*Arranged by* HANS UWE HIELSCHER

Hans U. Hielscher is represented in the U.S. by Artist Recitals, Los Angeles

F0649

Swell/Choir: Strings (Cel.) 8', 4', Sw./Ch.

(No transition if played as a separate piece.)

# SOMEBODY'S KNOCKIN' AT YOUR DOOR

Traditional
*Arranged by* HANS UWE HIELSCHER

(No transition if played
as a separate piece.)

# DEEP RIVER

Traditional
*Arranged by* HANS UWE HIELSCHER

F0649

Exclusively Distributed By

HAL•LEONARD®
CORPORATION
7777 W. BLUEMOUND RD. P.O. BOX 13819 MILWAUKEE, WI 53213